SPOOKY TUNES

Songs and Activities
by Don Cooper

Illustrated by Frank Daniel

Random House New York

Copyright © 1990 by Random House, Inc. All rights reserved under International and Pan-American Copyright Conventions. Published in the United States by Random House, Inc., New York, and simultaneously in Canada by Random House of Canada Limited, Toronto. ISBN: 0-679-80303-3 (pkg.)

All music and lyrics by Don Cooper. Lyrics copyright © 1990 by New Mutant Music. Illustrations copyright © 1990 by Frank Daniel. All rights reserved. Manufactured in the United States of America 1 2 3 4 5 6 7 8 9 10

Spooky Tunes

Chorus:

Spooky, scary ghosts and goblins,
Monsters, creepy, crawly things.
Spooky tunes don't cause me problems,
There's nothing I like better
Than a spooky song to sing.
There's nothing I like better
Than a spooky song to sing.

It's late at night, the moon is bright,
And I am wide awake.
I ask my dad to sing a spooky tune
To make me shake.
My stomach fills with butterflies,
My hair stands up on end,
And though I stare with frightened eyes,
I know it's just pretend.

(Repeat chorus)

I pull my blanket overhead,
Still, I can't help but peek
To see what's hiding 'neath my bed.
Sometimes I want to shriek!
I shiver and I quiver,
But I know the song's not through,
Until my heart goes boom-boom-boom!
When Daddy hollers, "Boo!"

(Repeat chorus twice)

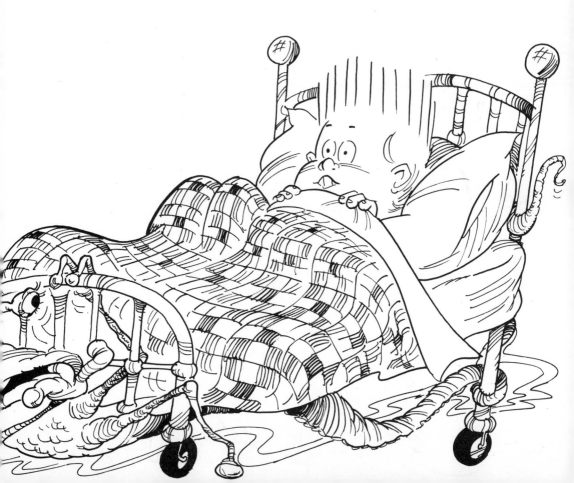

Spooky Clues

Q: Why was the skeleton afraid to cross the road?

A: Because he didn't have any ___ ___ ___ ___ !

Q: What do you get when you cross a bell with a bat?

A: A ___ ___ ___ ___ ___ ___ ___ !

In our secret code each symbol stands for a letter. Use the key below and put the right letters in the blanks to find the answers to these riddles.

Ghoul School

Ghoul school, ghoul school,
Dreary slime and drool school.
We'll learn to be creepy and weird and gross,
You be a zombie, I'll be a ghost.
Let's terrorize our ghoul schoolroom.
Here's a surprise, "The Voice of Doom!"
If you'll be a witch, I'll be your broom,
It's wickedly cool to be ghouls!
It's wickedly cool to be ghouls!

I want to be like Dracula,
A vampire in the night!
I want to be a Mummy,
Are my bandages wrapped right?
I'll be Dr. Jekyll, then I'll change to Mr. Hyde.
I want to be so scary,
Everyone will run and hide!

(Repeat first verse)

Silly School!

This school is not only ghoulish, it's also just plain foolish! Find the 8 silly things in the picture below.

Mr. Bones

Chorus:

Have you seen that skeleton,
The one called Mr. Bones?
You'll know it's him, he's the one with no skin,
The one who chatters and moans.
He rambles about with no insides or out,
Like a house built without any walls.
But you needn't be wary, though not ordinary,
He's really not scary at all.
You needn't be wary, though not ordinary,
He's really not scary at all!

Clickety-clackety, clappety-snap,
I recognize those tones.
It's that body-less one, that skeleton,
Who's known as Mr. Bones.
I heard him one night when the moon was bright;
I crept to my backyard to spy.
I heard his joints creaking, so nervously speaking,
"Show yourself, bone-man," said I.
"Up here," he answered. I lifted my glance—
There he was in a tree, plain as day!
In a voice like cold metal he croaked,
"Little fellow, is it safe?
Have the dogs gone away?"

(Repeat chorus)

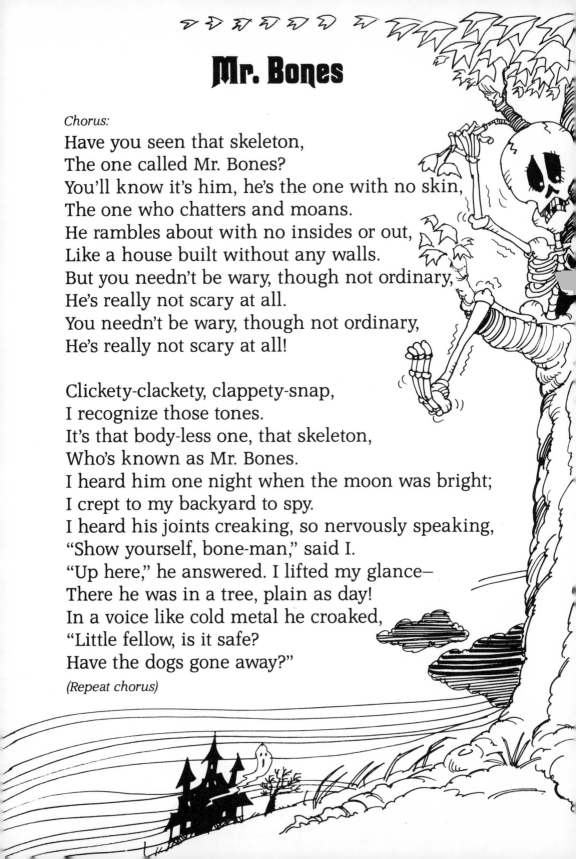

I understood that a skeleton would be
A snack for a dog when he groaned:
"There's nothing I hate worse
Than that oft-refrained verse,
Give the poor doggie a bone!
There is nothing so scrumptious
For a dog who feels munchous,
As a skeleton walking alone!"

(Repeat chorus)

As he rambled away, I heard Mr. Bones say,
"If you're walking through swamps or through bogs
And you hear a strange noise,
It's skeletons, boys and girls,
Running away from the dogs!"

(Repeat chorus)

Give the Dog a Bone!

It looks as though Fido caught Mr. Bones and hid him all over the yard! Can you find the six hidden bones in the picture below?

The Witch Way

Get a fat black cat, get a tall black hat.
Find a broom to fly you through the sky, hooray!
There's really nothing to it—
Simply twitch your nose and do it this way.
Which way? The witch way!

Get a long black dress, make your hair a mess.
You will scare your friends
And family when you say,
"By the pricking of my thumb,
I'm sure that something wicked's coming this way."
Which way? The witch way!

Get a crystal ball and look into the future.
Suit yourself, you may prefer
To view the past or in between.
Weave a few black magic spells,
Or brew a spooky stew which smells so bad
Your neighbors all will scream, "Good grief!"
Believe me...

(Repeat first verse, then third verse, and first verse again.)

Which Witch Is Which?

Two of the witches below are the same. Can you find them?

Cat-astrophe!

When these witches went cat walking,
everything got all tangled up! Follow the lines
to find out which cats belong to which witch.

Spooky Stew

Great green gobs of greasy,
Grimy gopher guts,
Scabs from scratches, bumps, and cuts,
Yuck! It sounds disgusting, but
Just throw them in your
Trusty, rusty, crusty pot,
And boo! It's Spooky Stew.

Bat wings, cat screams,
Slimy worms and spider webs,
Lizard legs and lopped-off heads,
Dust balls from beneath your bed.
Stir them up and quick
As any witch has said,
"Boo!" It's Spooky Stew.

YUM! YUM!

OUT TO LUNCH

TODAY'S SPECIAL
SPOOKY STEW

Ghouls say you can't beat it.
It would take a *fool* to eat it.
Holy smoke, I hope it's just pretend!
If a restaurant I went to
Had it offered on its menu,
I would scream and leave,
And not go back again!

Add a dash of doggie breath and moldy bones,
Swampy water, sticks and stones,
Season it with shrieks and moans.
It's so gross, a ghost would probably gag
And groan, "Ooooh, that's Spooky Stew!"

(Repeat last two verses)

EXIT

The Cauldron
Nasty Cuisine!

What's Cooking?

If you were going to make Spooky Stew, what would you put in the pot? Draw lines from the *spooky* ingredients to the inside of the pot.

Hidden Horror!

There's something scary hidden in the picture below. Color in all the shapes that have a dot to find out what it is.

You Look Terrible!

"You look terrible!"
    "Nice of you to say."
"Horrible, unbearable!"
    "I'm trying to look that way."
"Your face could crack a mirror!"
        "Then get a mirror, let's crack away!
        I confess that I'm just dressed up
        For this spooky holiday."

Chorus:

Halloween, I'll paint my face up,
Halloween, with colored gook.
Halloween, I'm going to dress up
In a costume like a spook.
And when I go trick or treating,
At each doorbell that I touch,
When they tell me I look terrible!
I'll say, "Thank you very much!"
When they tell me, "You look terrible!"
I'll say, "Thank you very much!"

"You look ghastly!"
    "You're really much too kind."
"Ghostly! Nasty!"
    "It took a long, long time."
"You're a sight to make my stomach turn!"
        "Well, please don't turn away—
        'Cause stomach turning's half the fun
        This spooky holiday!"

(Repeat chorus twice)

Monster Makeup

Some costumes have masks, but people also use monster makeup to make themselves look scary. Color the faces below and turn them into monsters!

Do the Bogeyman

Kids, I'm called the Bogeyman.
I suppose you're wondering why.
It's 'cause I do this bogey dance—
You want to have a try?
Oh, it's really very easy,
Lookee here, I'll show you how.
Just follow the directions that I sing.
Let's start right now!

Say boo! just like a Bogeyman.
Hey, you can do this bogey dance.
Make a scary face, then
Bend down at the waist,
Shake your body like the Bogeymen do!

Now laugh just like a Bogeyman.
You have to laugh and clap your hands.
If you can stick your tongue out very far,
You'll look real scary.
Chances are you'll scare the Bogeyman too!

Howl and holler *Bogeyman*!
Yes, now you've got the rhythm, man.
Lie down on the floor and kick your feet,
Then give a roar just like a lion.
That's what Bogeymen do!

Jump high, say "I'm the Bogeyman!"
Spin round and round till you can't stand.
Chances are you'll fall down giggling,
But if you can just keep wiggling,
You can be a Bogeyman too!

Make believe you're wild and hairy.
Do this dance real fast and scary—
And you can be a Bogeyman too!

Spooky Riddle Time

Q: Why is this baby monster crying?

A: Because he misses his M __ __ __ __ !

Circle every third stepping stone on the path below, starting with the letter M. Fill in the blanks with the circled letters and solve this spooky riddle.

So You Want to Be a Monster?

Draw a picture of what you would look like if you were a monster, then print your name on the line below it!

_____, the Monster!

The Haunted House

On a hill outside of town,
Nestled 'neath the whispering pines,
There stood an old, old house they claimed was haunted.
Its porch was broken down
And the yard was full of vines.
It was exactly like the old ghost wanted.

There were cobwebs in the corners
And the windowpanes were cracked.
There were bats up in the attic
And the doors were painted black.
When you opened them, they squeaked and groaned,
Then slammed shut with a *WHACK*!
It was exactly where a ghost would play!

Chorus:
Ooh, ooh, ooh, ooh, ooh, ooh, ooh!
Every old ghost needs a place to stay.
Ooh, ooh, ooh, ooh, ooh, ooh, ooh!
I only make these sounds to scare
The human beings away!

It was a mondo condominium,
As quiet as a mouse.
T'was nothing there a human being would care for.
And when that old ghost moved in there,
It became a haunted house.
He had a musty, dusty, fusty home to scare
    and care for!

(Repeat chorus twice)

The Amazing Haunted House!

Help find the safe path through the Haunted House.

Fright Night!

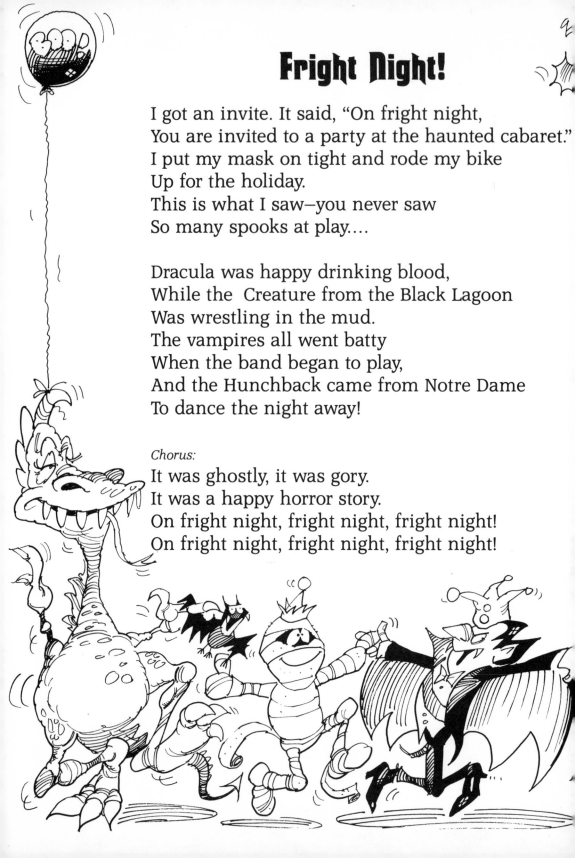

I got an invite. It said, "On fright night,
You are invited to a party at the haunted cabaret."
I put my mask on tight and rode my bike
Up for the holiday.
This is what I saw—you never saw
So many spooks at play....

Dracula was happy drinking blood,
While the Creature from the Black Lagoon
Was wrestling in the mud.
The vampires all went batty
When the band began to play,
And the Hunchback came from Notre Dame
To dance the night away!

Chorus:

It was ghostly, it was gory.
It was a happy horror story.
On fright night, fright night, fright night!
On fright night, fright night, fright night!

All the witches checked their broomsticks at the door.
When the band played loud, it pleased the crowd,
And the werewolves howled for more.
Frankenstein and old King Kong danced the boogaloo.
And even though they liked the songs,
The ghosts all hollered, "Boo!"

(Repeat chorus)

The Mummy and the Wolfman shot the breeze.
Godzilla flapped his scaly tail,
And the goblins slapped their knees.
Then the ballroom clock struck midnight,
And I had to hurry home.
When the skeletons waved, "Good night, pal,"
They rattled all their bones.

(Repeat chorus)

ABC the Monster!

Connect the letters from A to Z to see what kind of monster is going to the Fright Night Ball!

Isn't It Fun to Be a Little Scared?

Isn't it fun the way we jump
When someone hollers, "Boo!"
And it's a laugh, the way we gasp
To think we've seen a ghoul!
Spooks are kooky, ghosts are goofy,
Even monsters like to fool around.
Oh, isn't it thrilling, this tingling in the air?
Isn't it fun to be a little scared?

Don't be frightened or afraid,
'Cause it's only make-believe.
What we're scared of in the dark
Are just the things that we can't see.
It's just our imagination playing tricks.
So why don't we imagine
Spooky things are really fun, and funny as can be!

Isn't it silly the way we shake
And shiver in our beds,
When monsters are really just creepy things
We make up in our heads.
It's excitin' to be frightened,
When it's all a game of ghost pretend.
Oh, isn't it thrilling, this feeling that we share?
Isn't it fun to be a little scared?
Isn't it fun to be a little scared?

Tricks and Treats

Here are some more ghostly games and creepy crafts, guaranteed to be monstrous fun!

1. Bone Jewelry
Paint pieces of macaroni white. When they are dry, string them on a piece of yarn or thread and tie them around your neck or wrist. When your friends ask you what they are, tell them that they're finger bones!

2. Spooky Cookies
Make your favorite rolled-cookie recipe, and chill the dough well. Slice the chilled dough into circles, then carefully use a butter knife to shape the dough into bats, cats, pumpkins, or anything you want! Decorate black cats with chocolate icing, pumpkins with orange icing, and ghosts with white icing or coconut.

3. Tissue-paper Terrors
Take two white tissues or paper towels. Crumple one up and place it in the middle of the other one. Gather the bottom tissue and fasten with string or a twist-tie to form a head. (See illustration.) Draw a face on the head, and presto! You've made a Tissue Terror! If you make four or five of them and hang them from a coat hanger, you have a ghost mobile! Or put the head over your finger and you have ghost finger puppets!